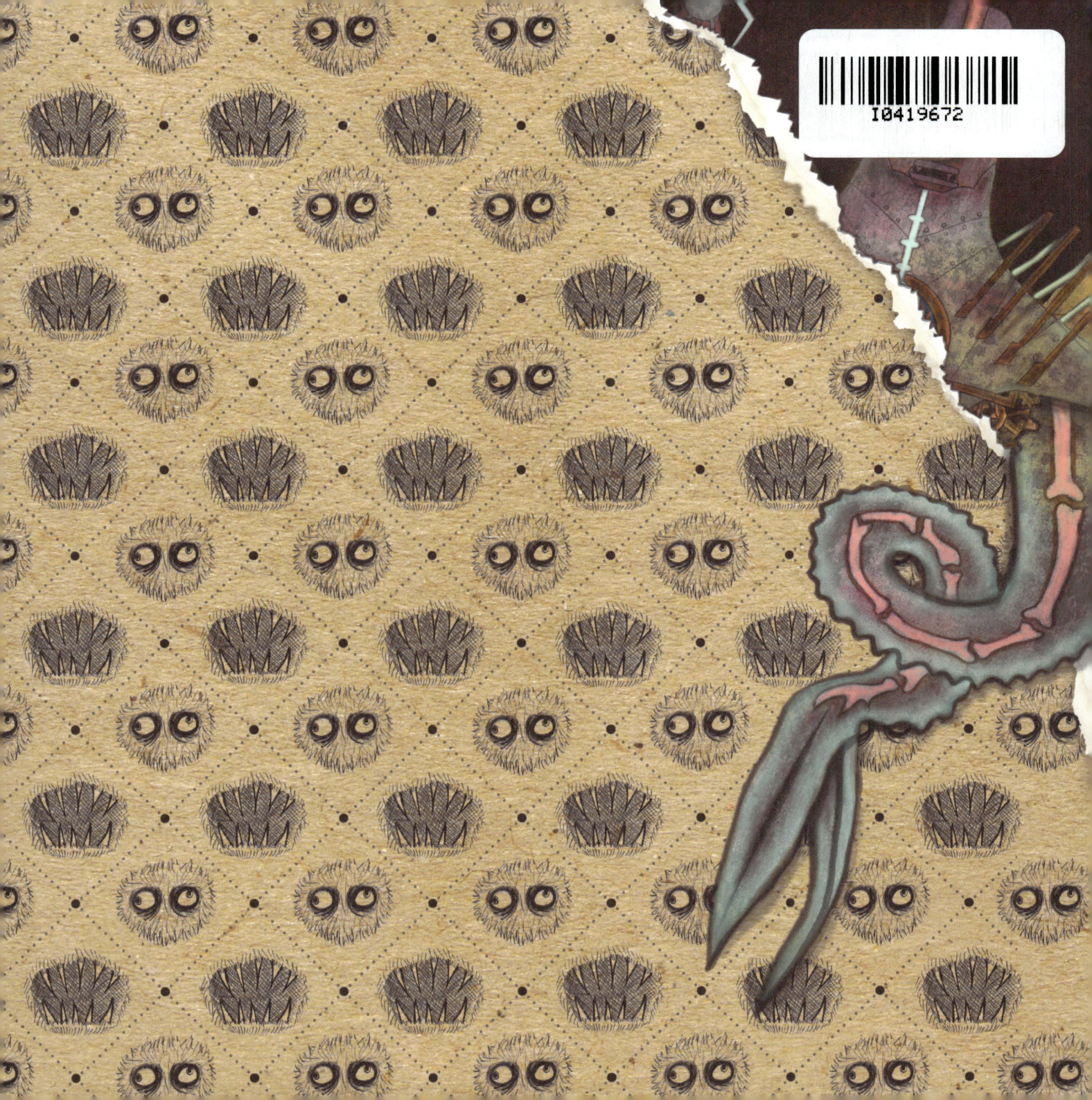

For those who see the world differently.

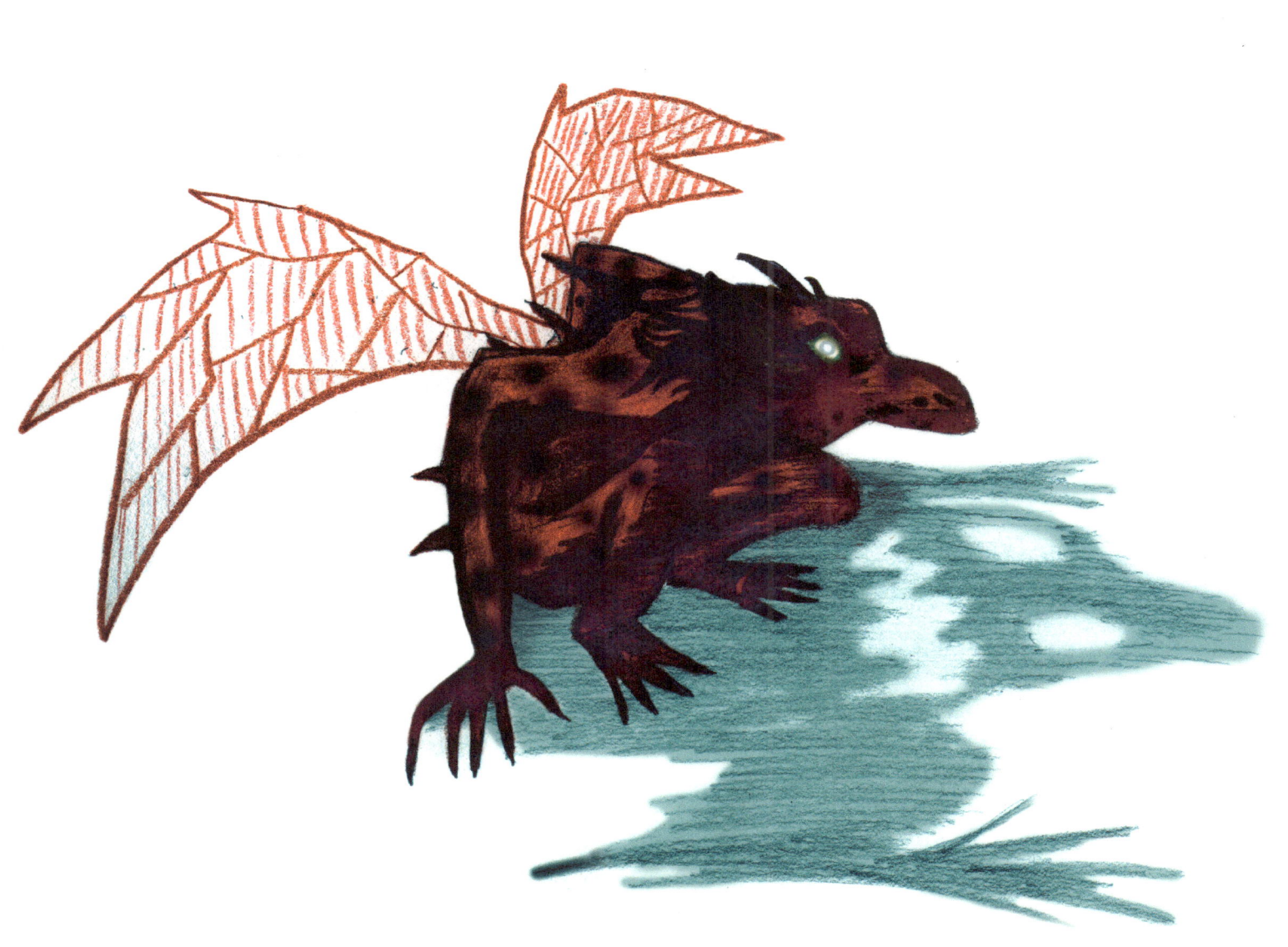

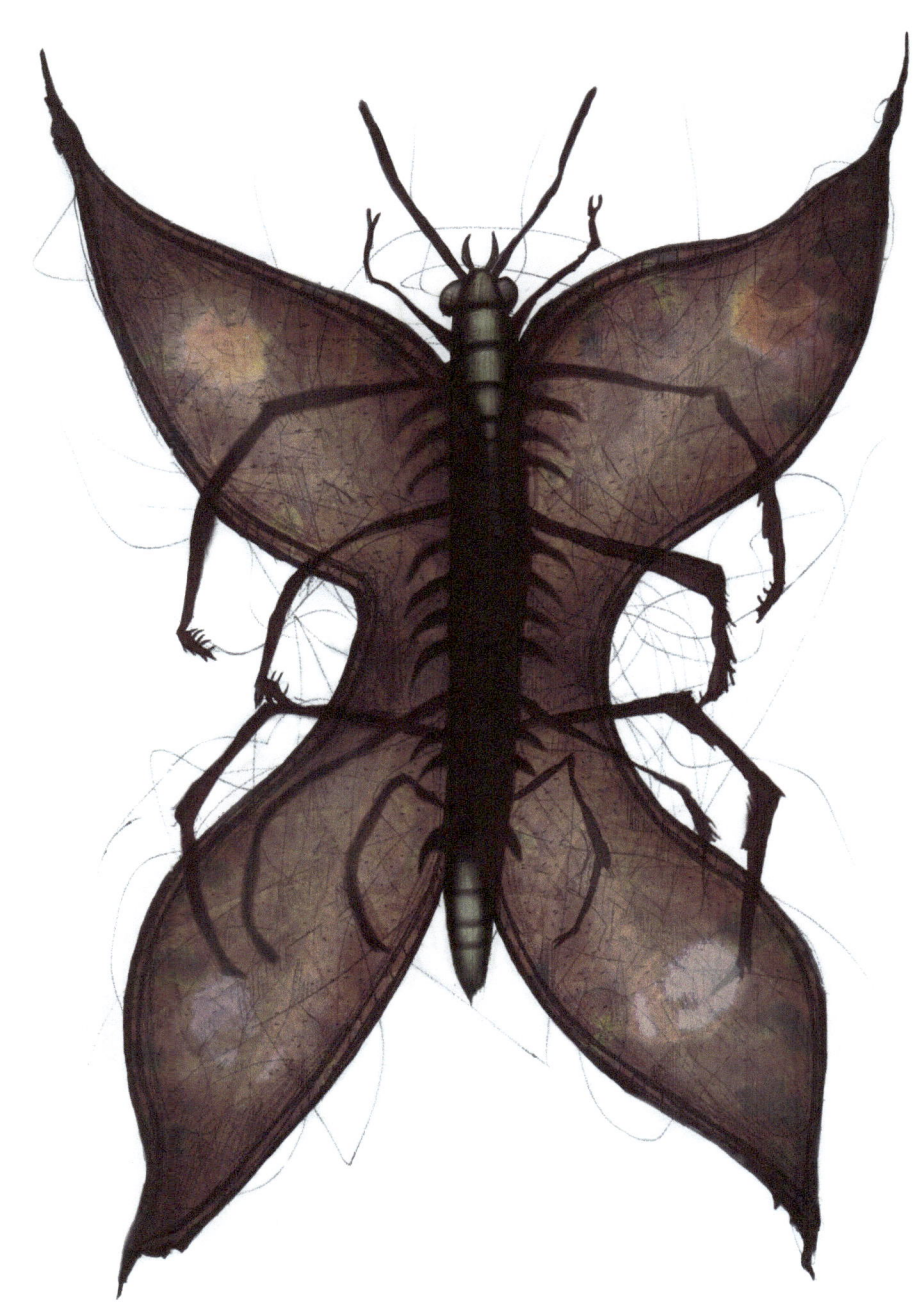

MONSTERS

by Dana Hocking

illustrated by Josh Funk

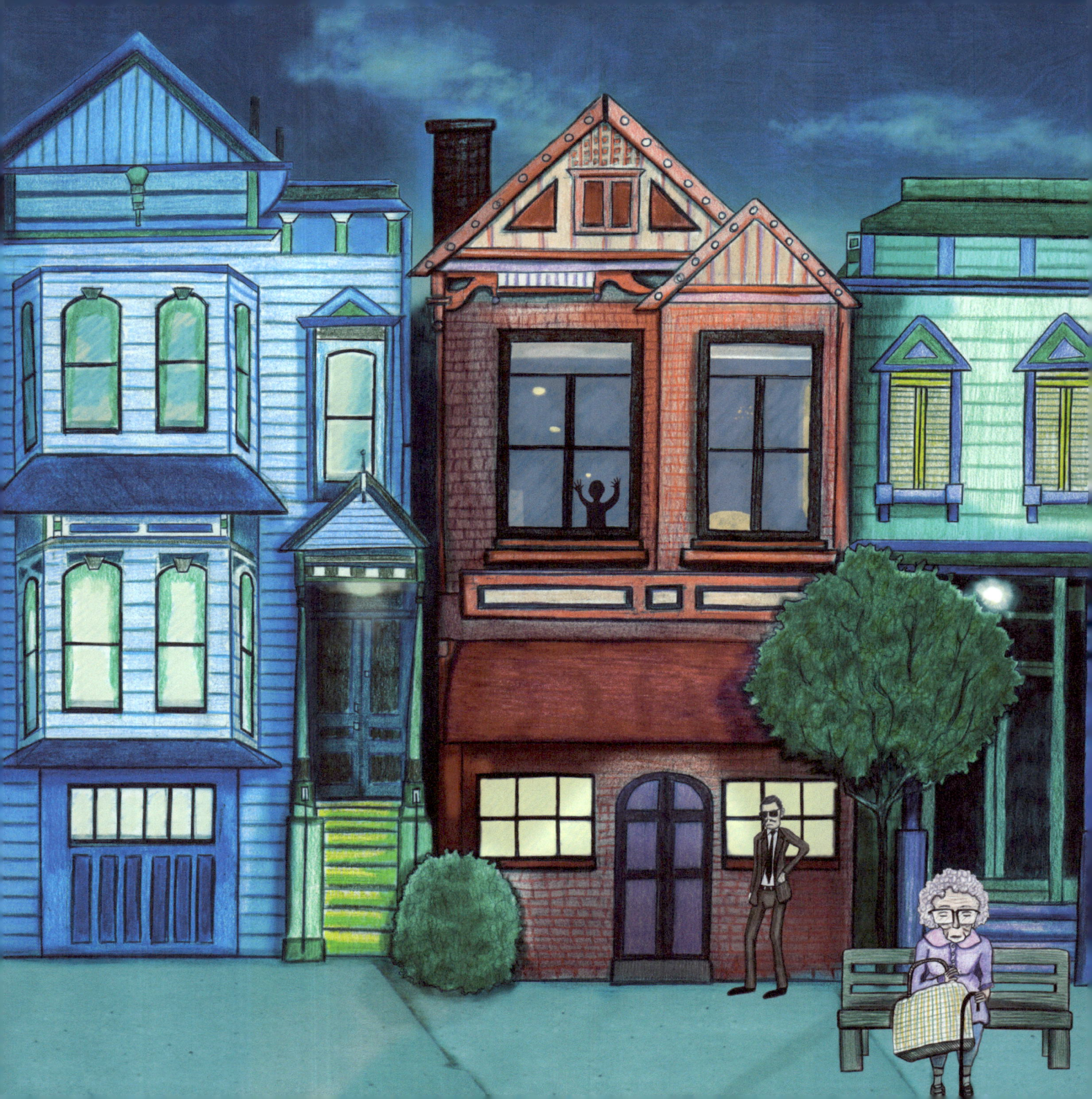

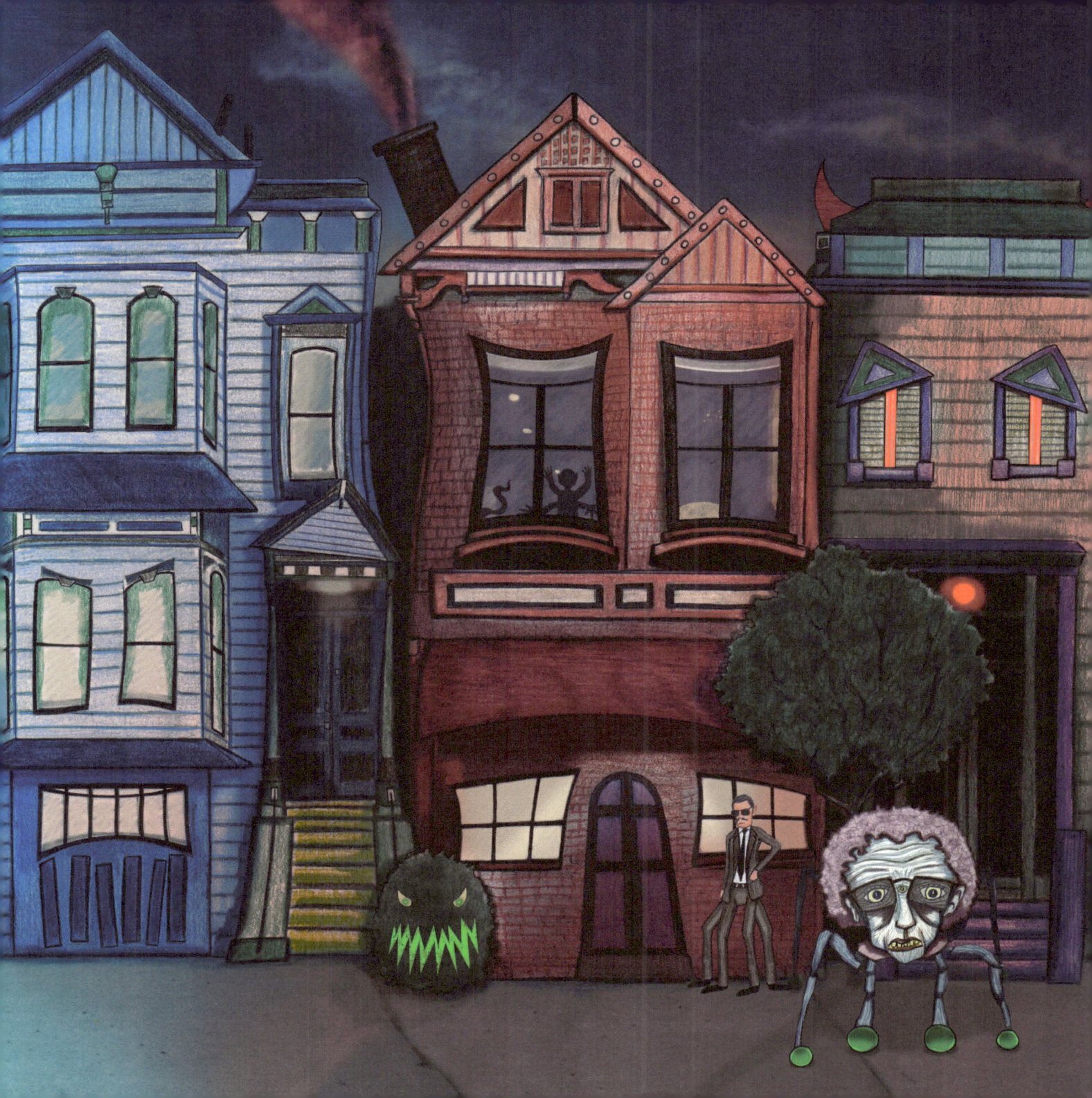

There is a different world than this.
It is the world of monsters.
It is the world we hide
from our children.
But they know it's there.

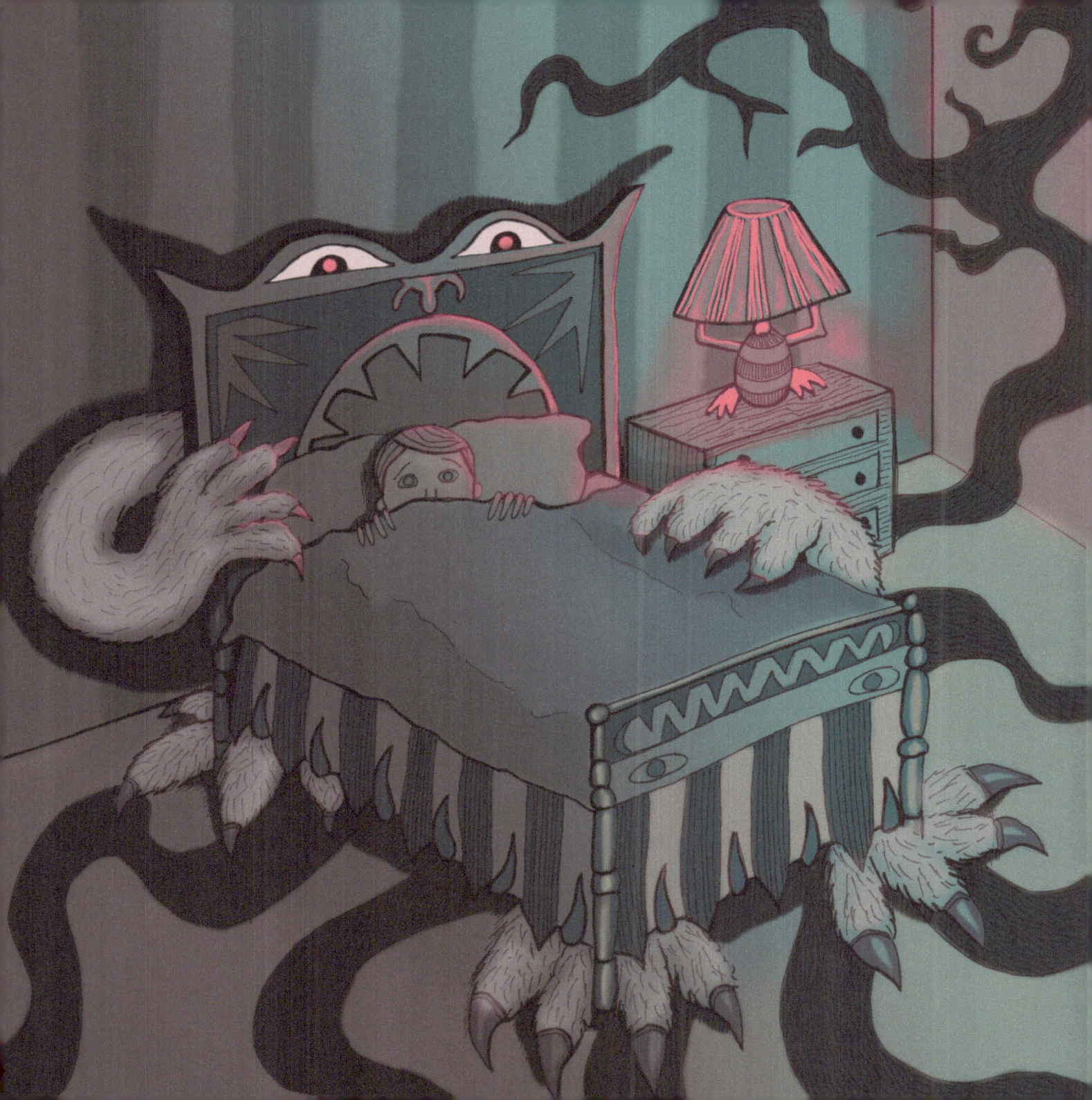

They are born knowing.
And then, over time,
they begin to forget.
Until eventually,
they start to believe
that it was never really there
in the first place.

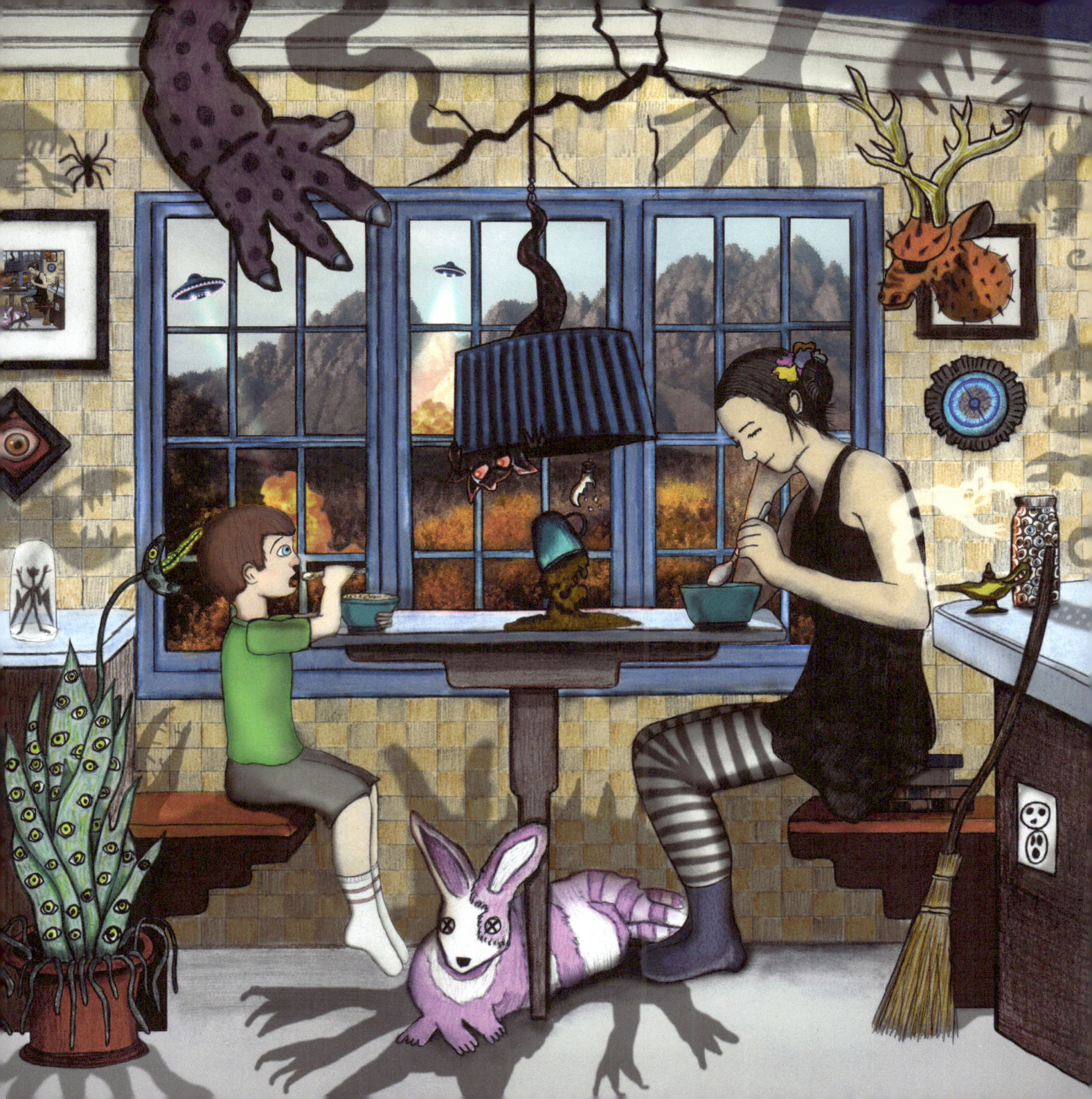

And we tell them they're right.
We tell them it was all in their minds.

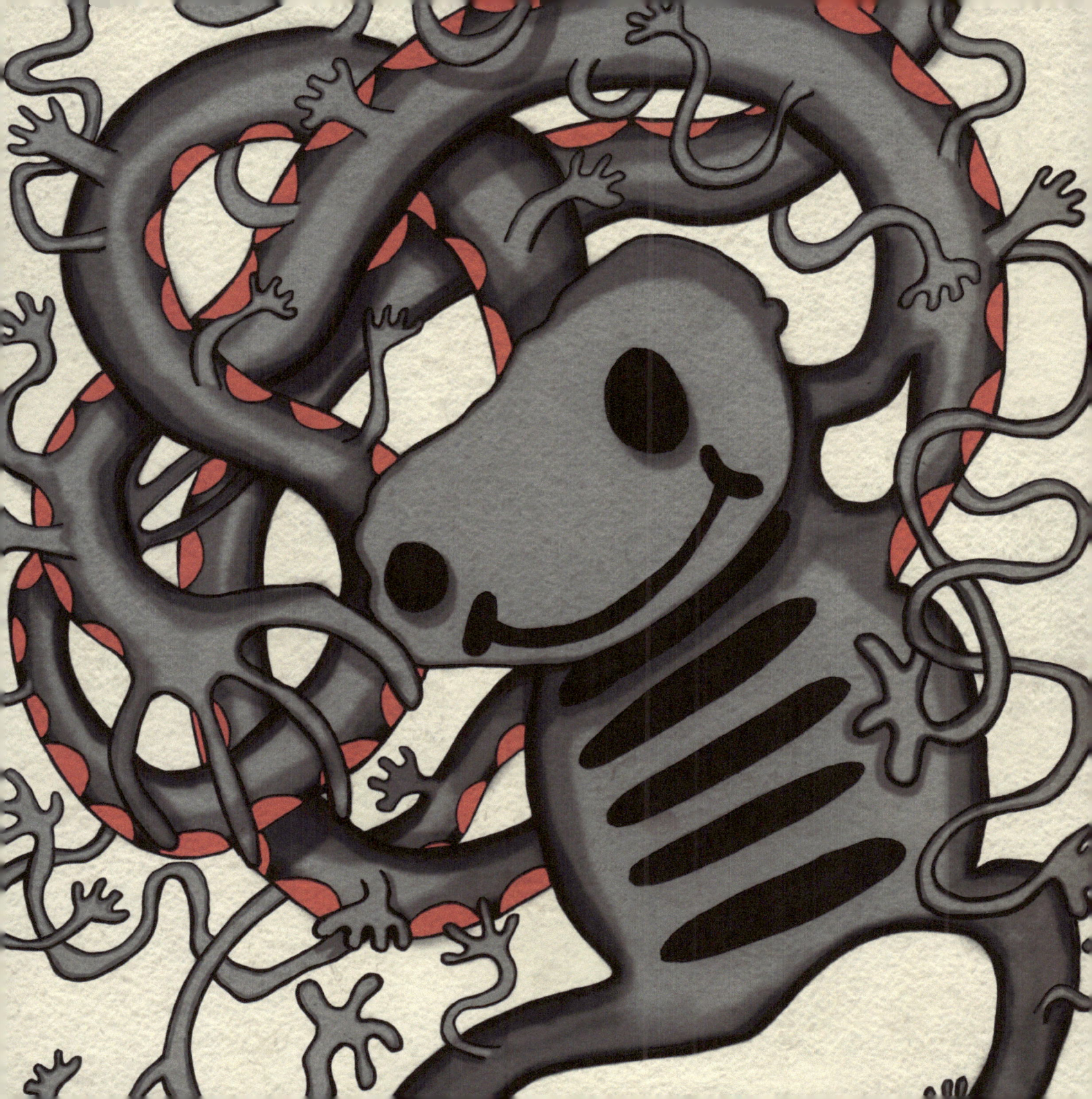

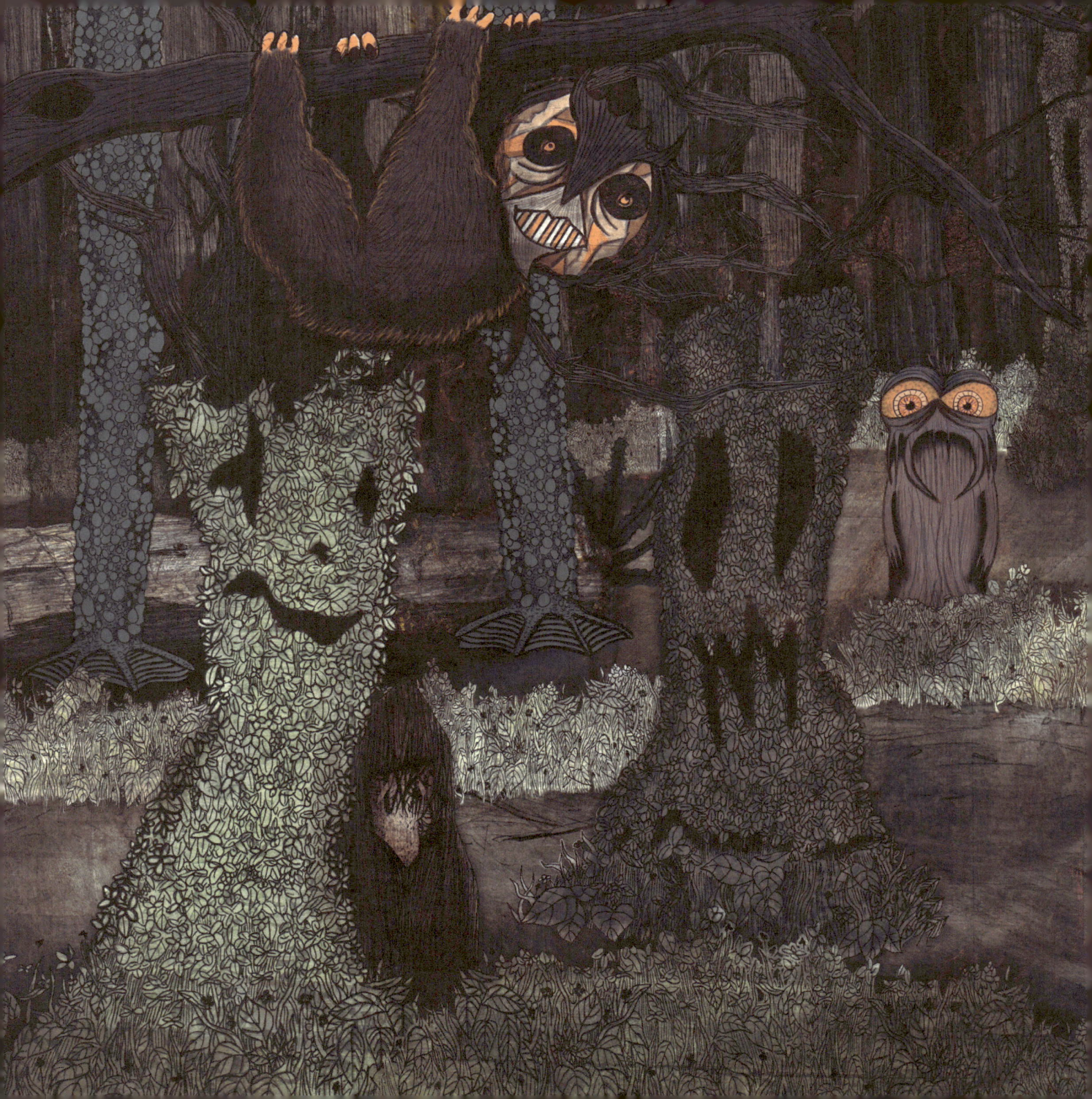

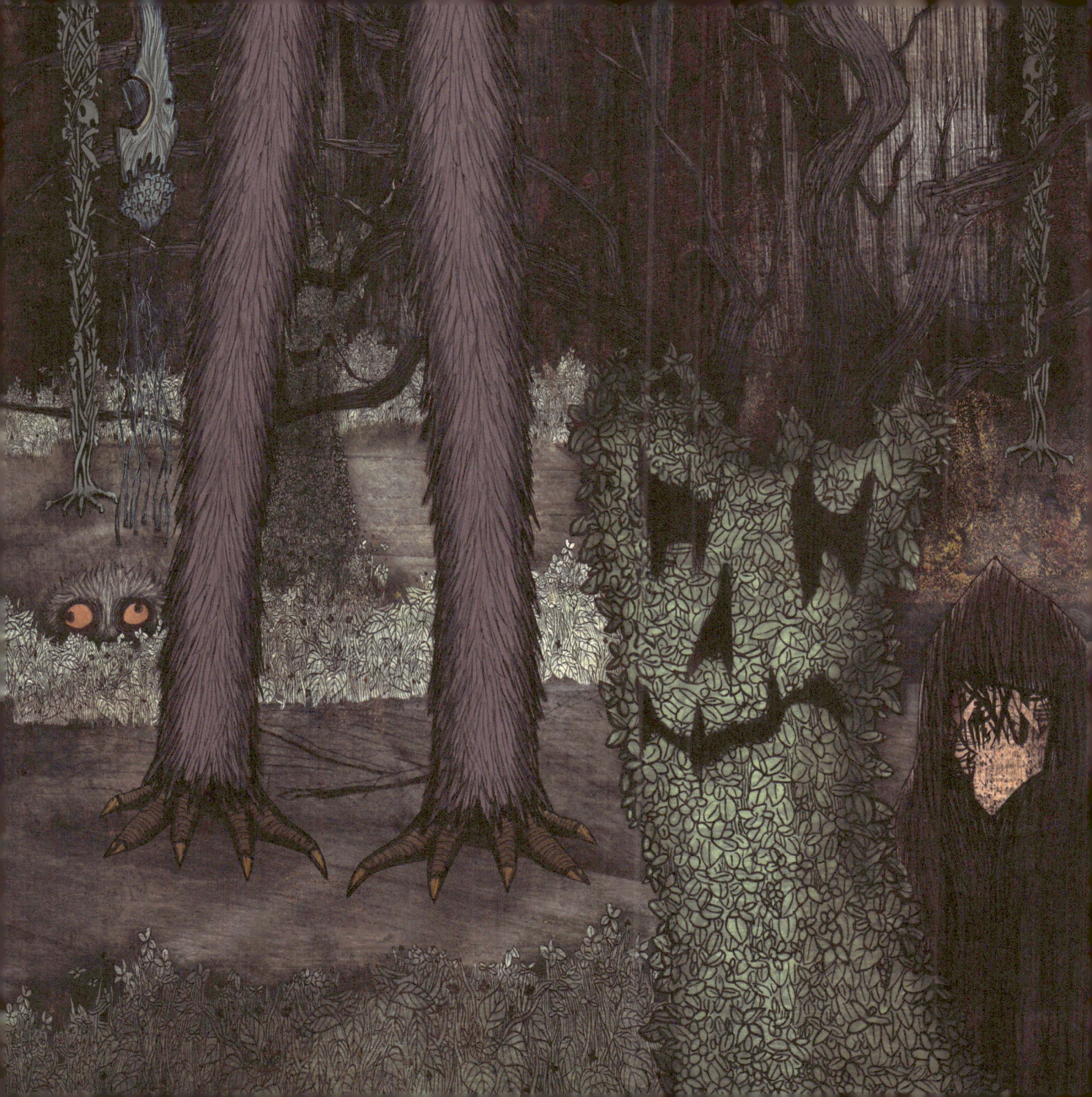

But there are anomalies.

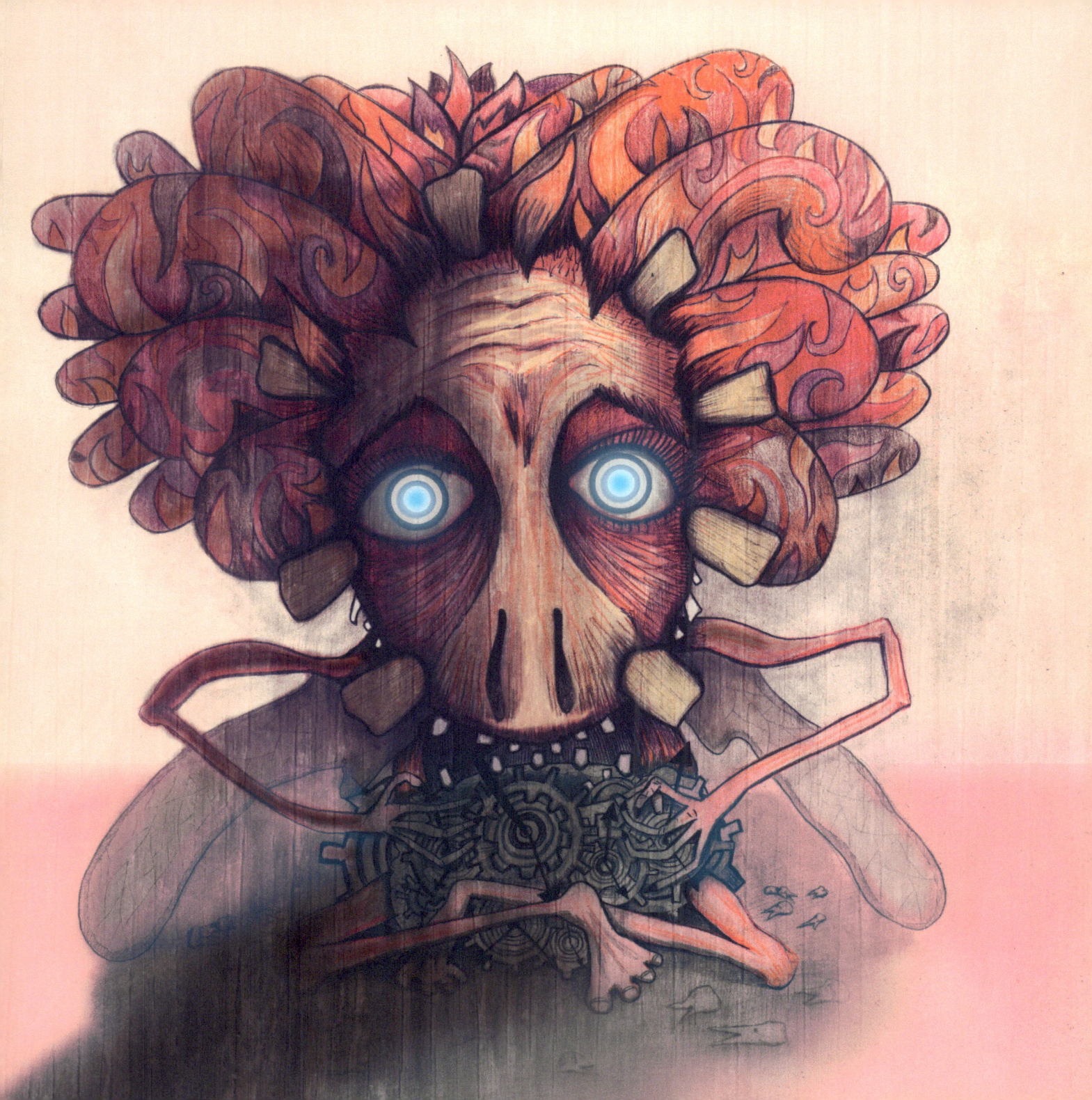

There are those who figure out
how to see that world again.
And some of them
document what they find.

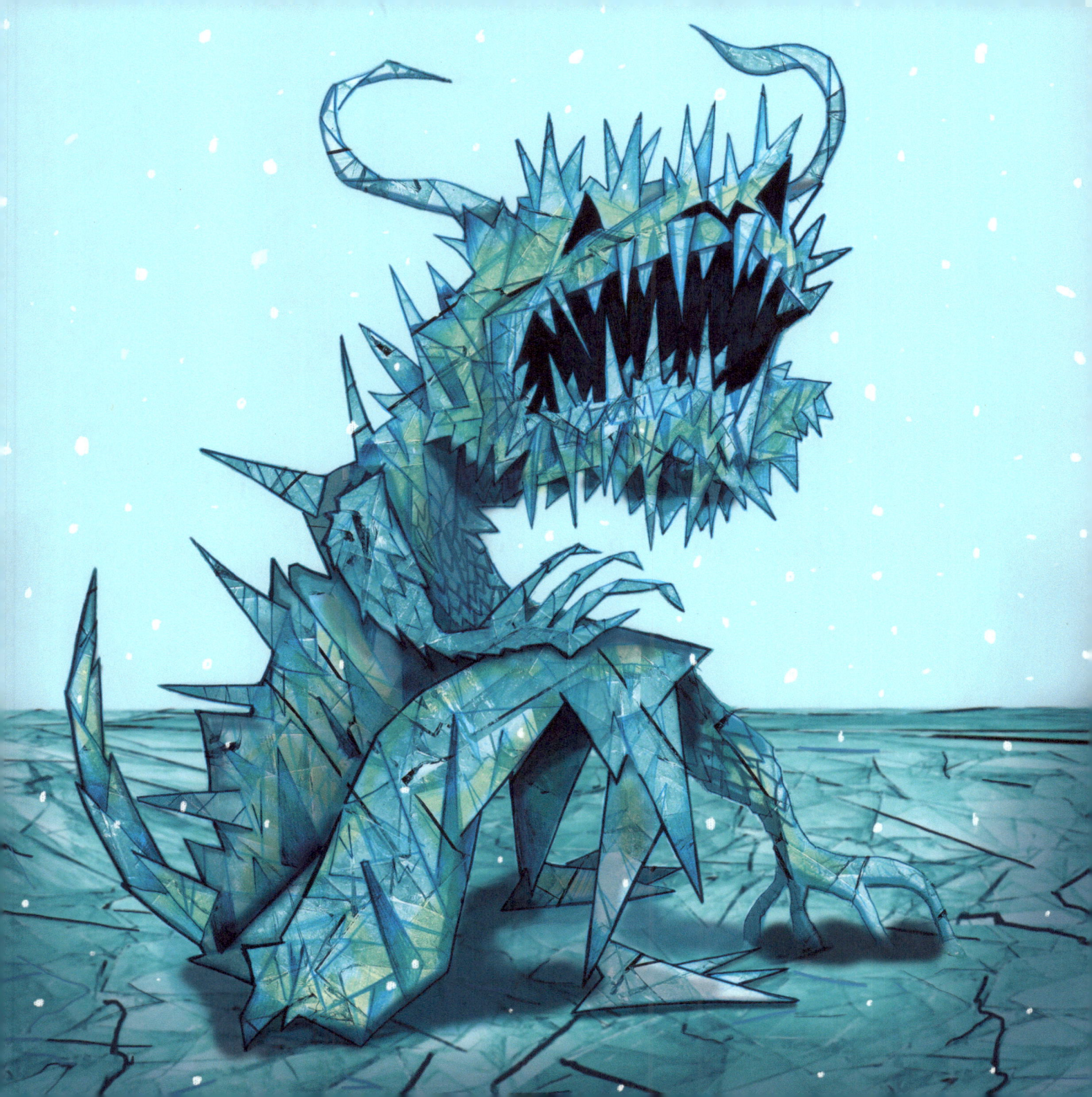

Decide for yourself, but be careful.
Once you know, you can't unknow.

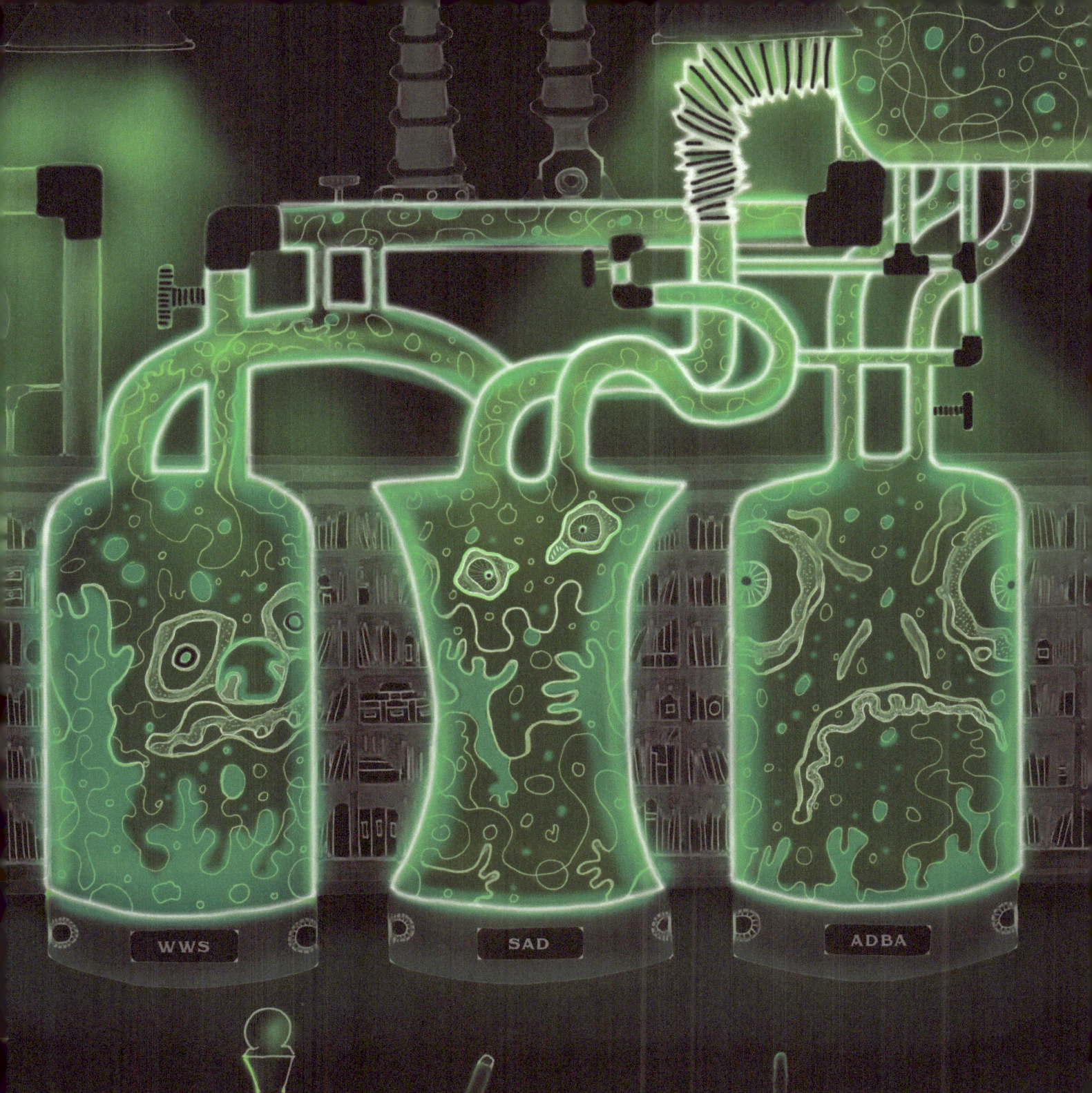

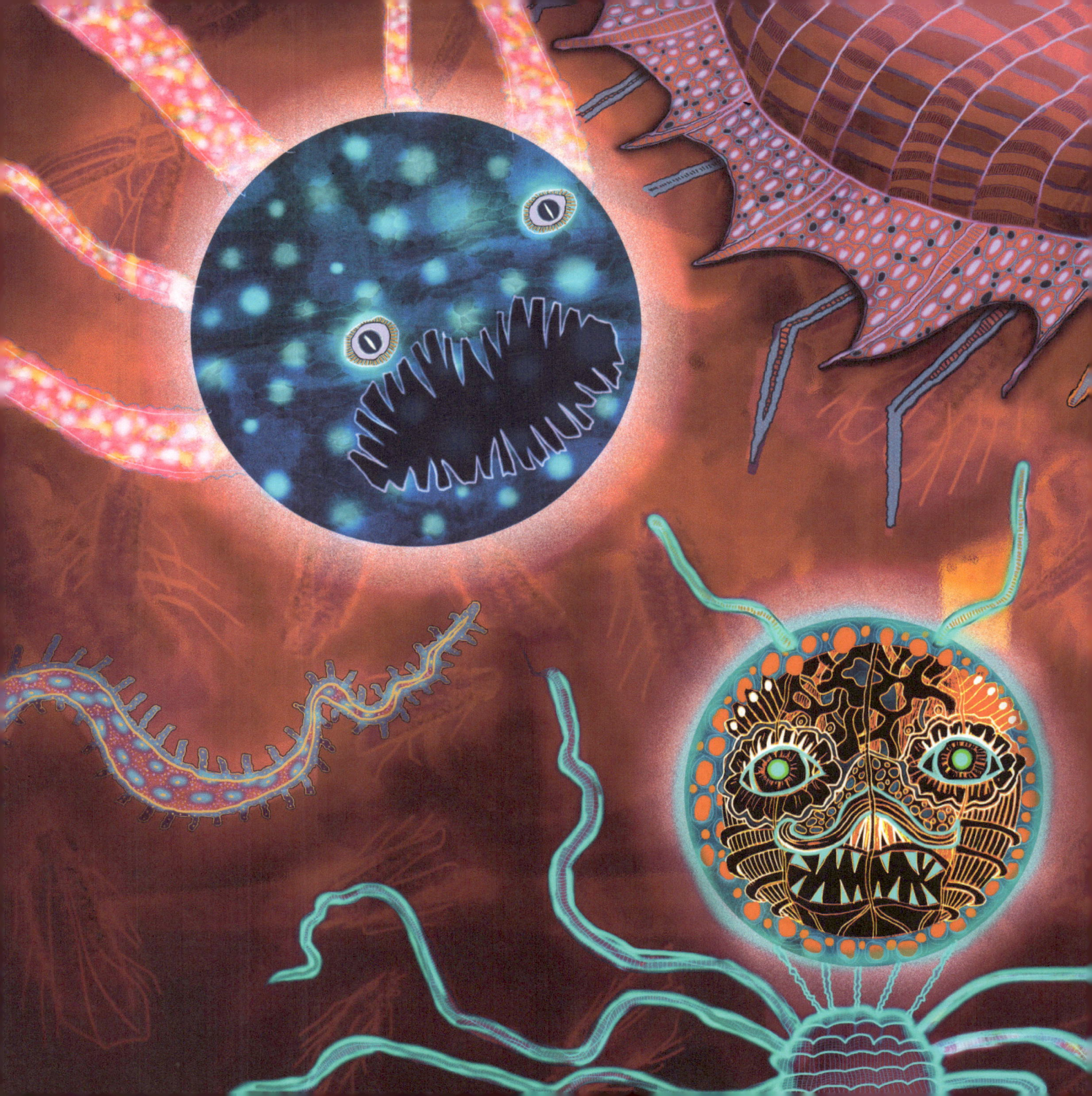

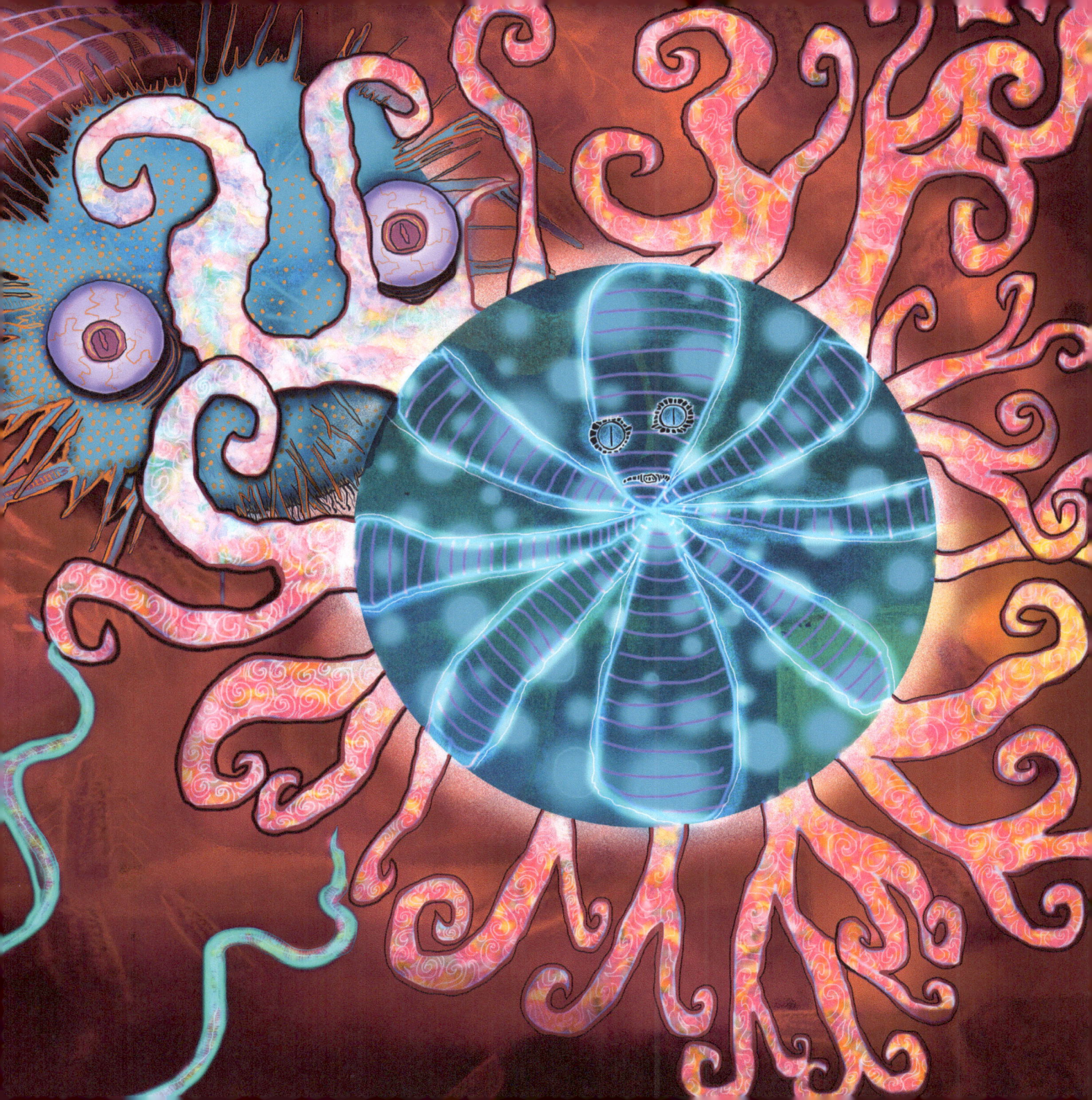

Eventually, they know.

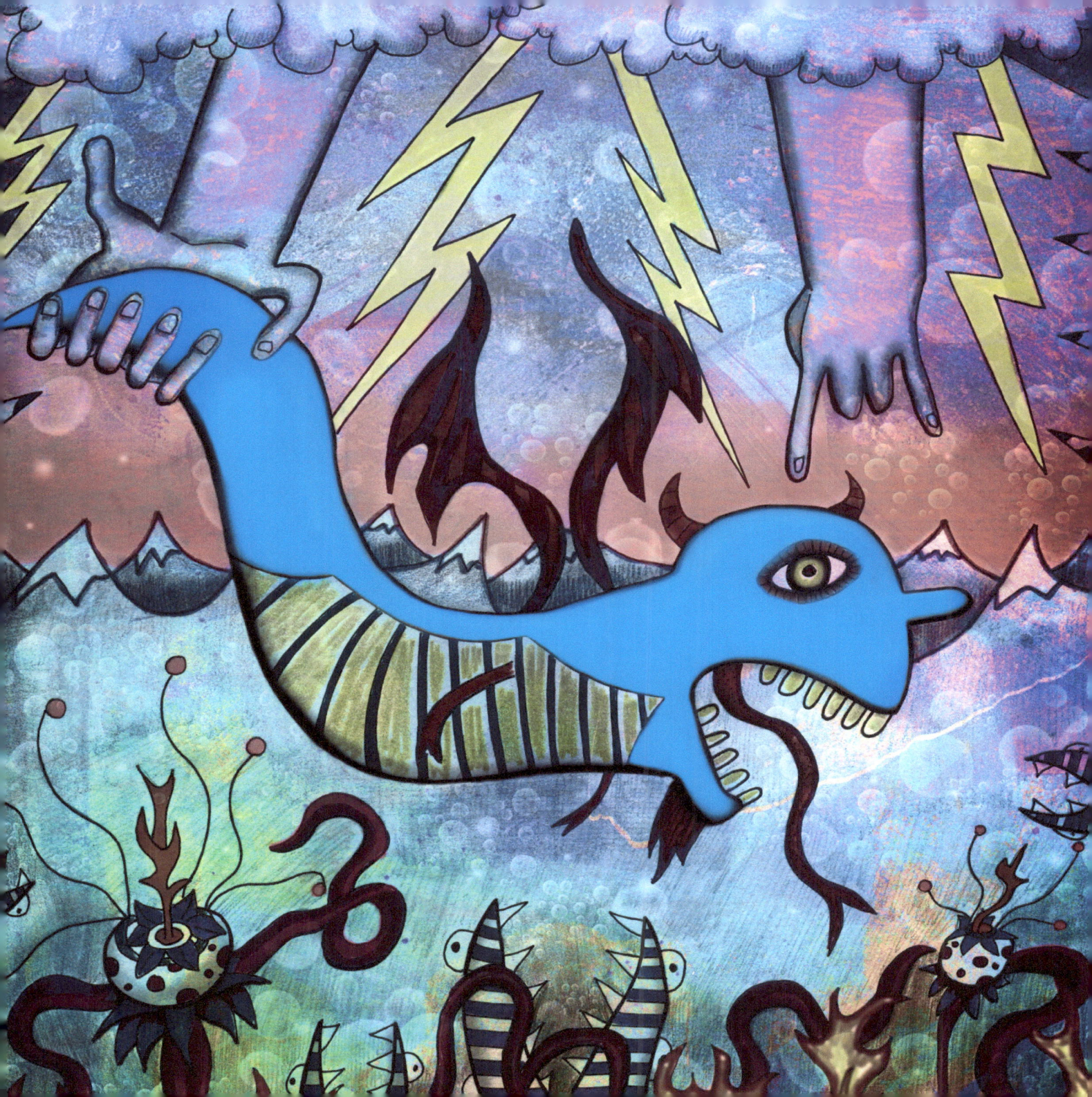

And when that happens,
they no longer try to
convince us that they know.
They can't unknow.
So it doesn't matter.

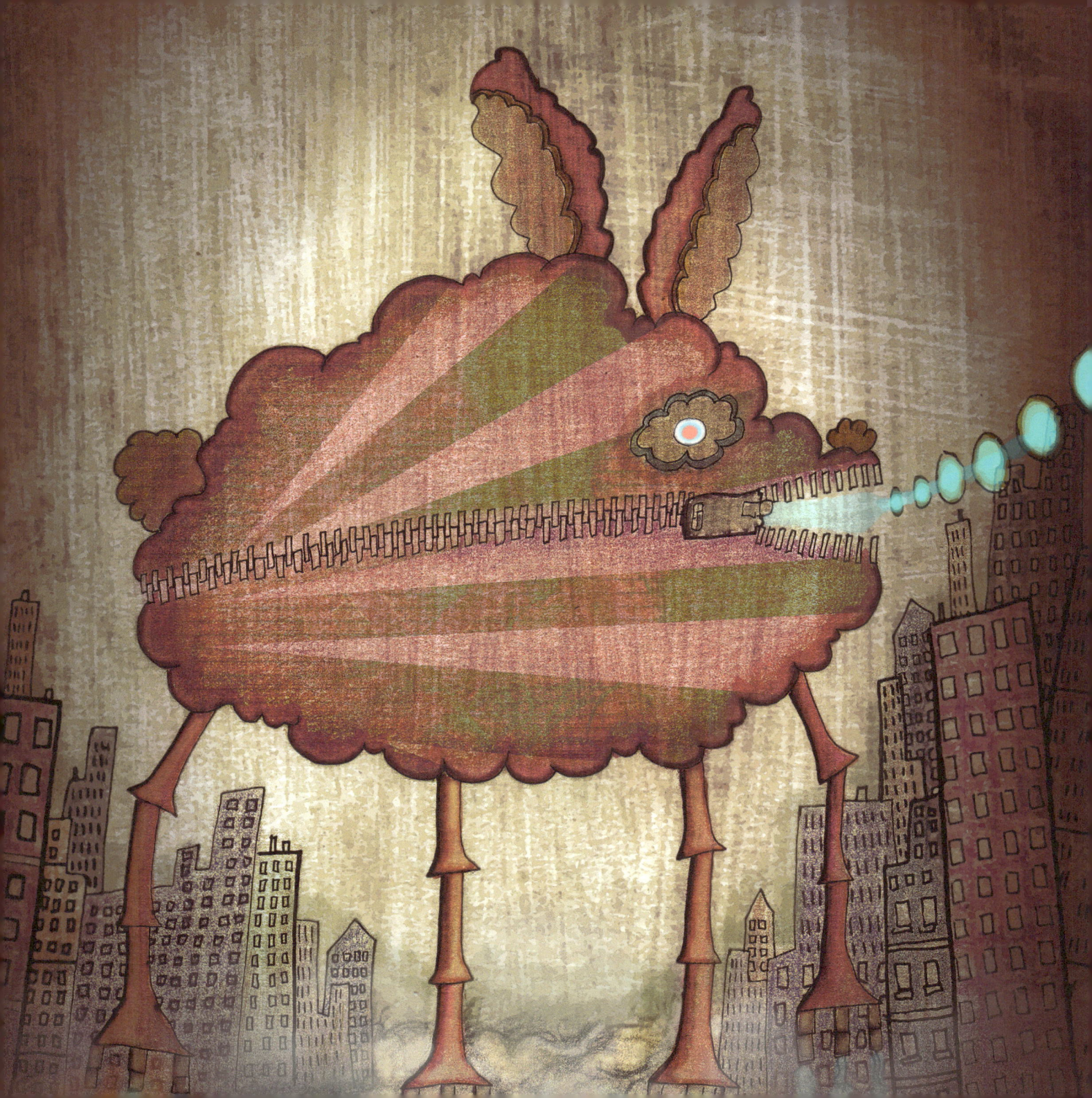

And then there are no more secrets.

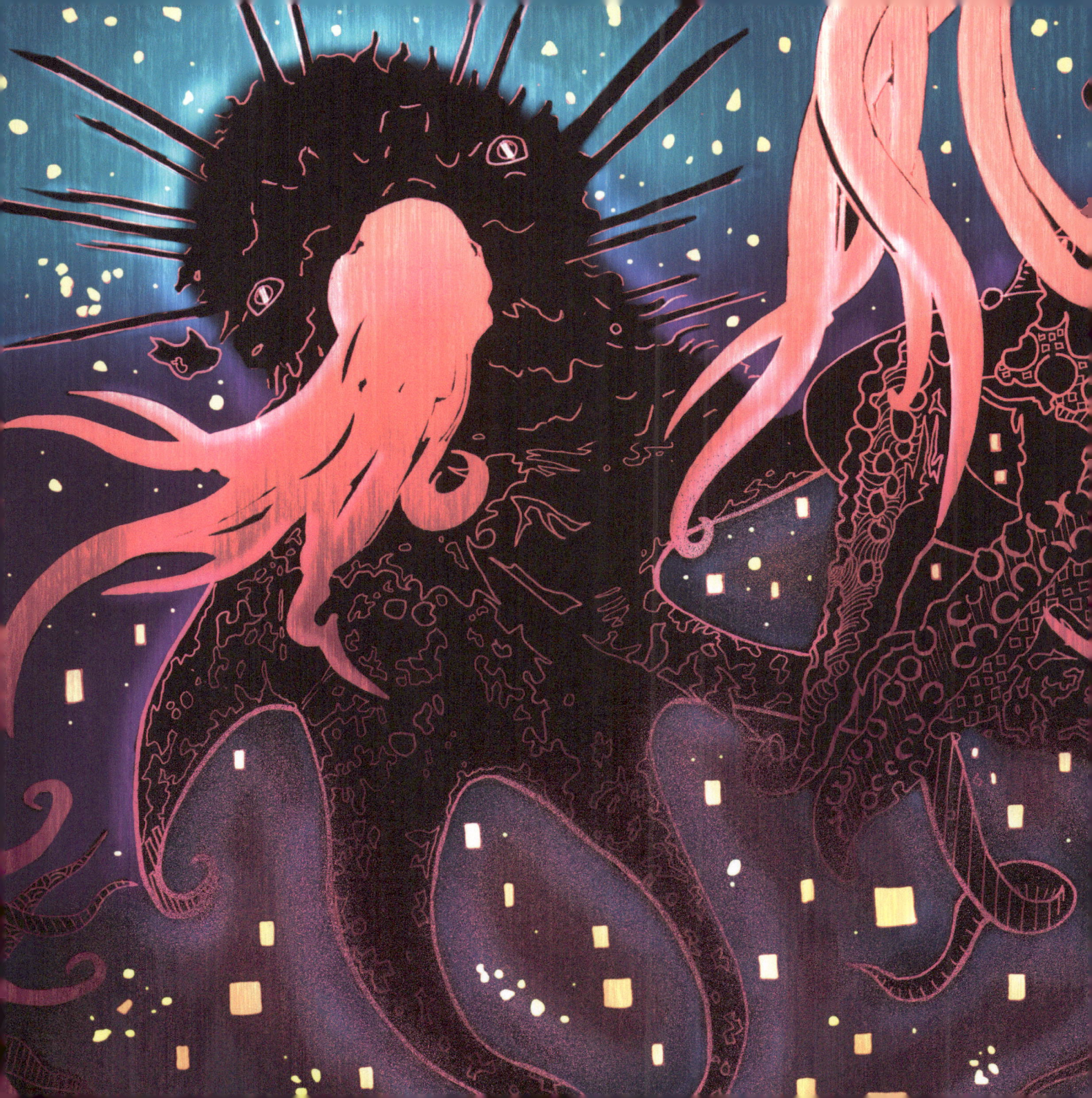

And then there is no more hiding.

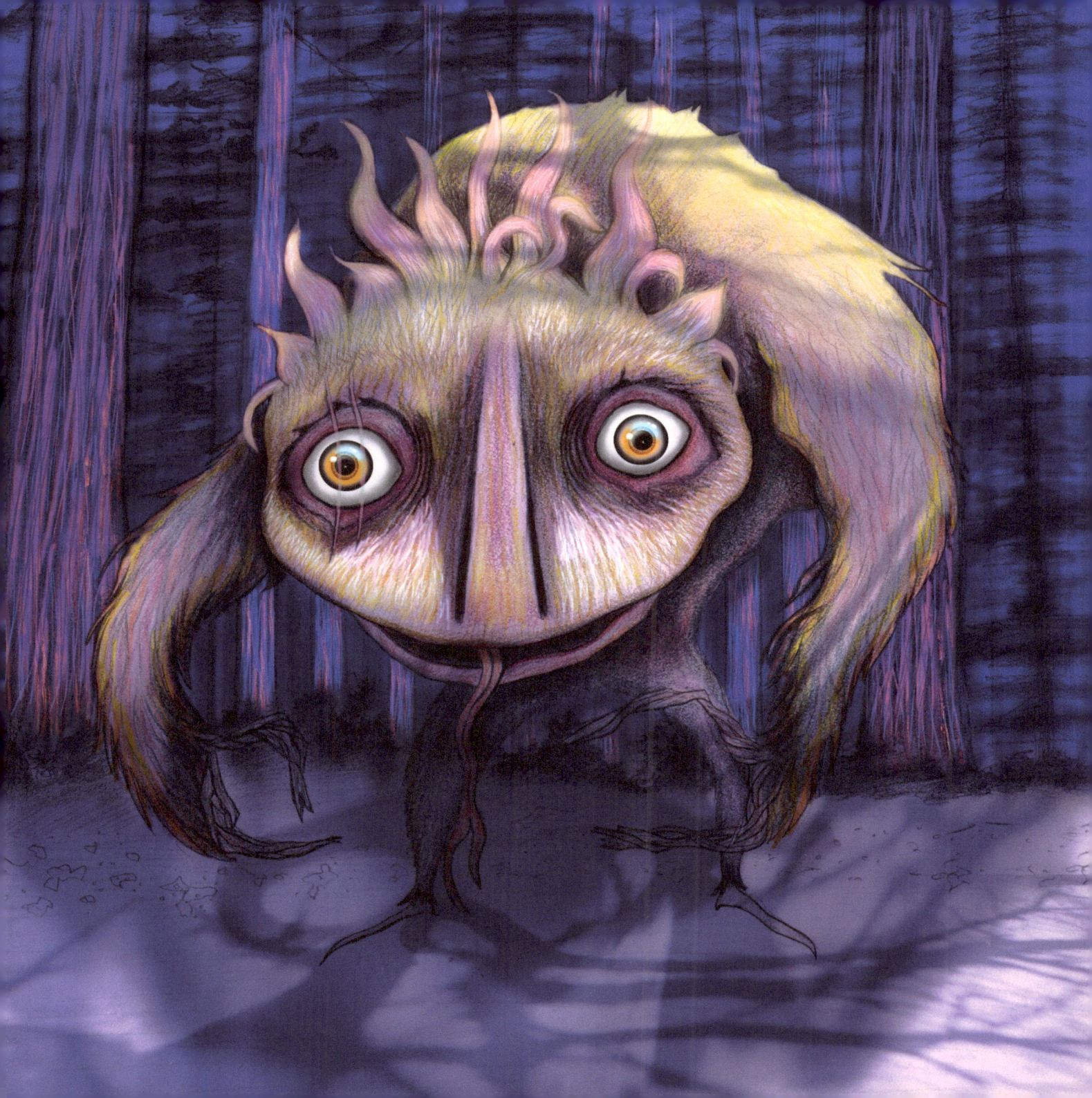

So, finally, we tell them we know too.

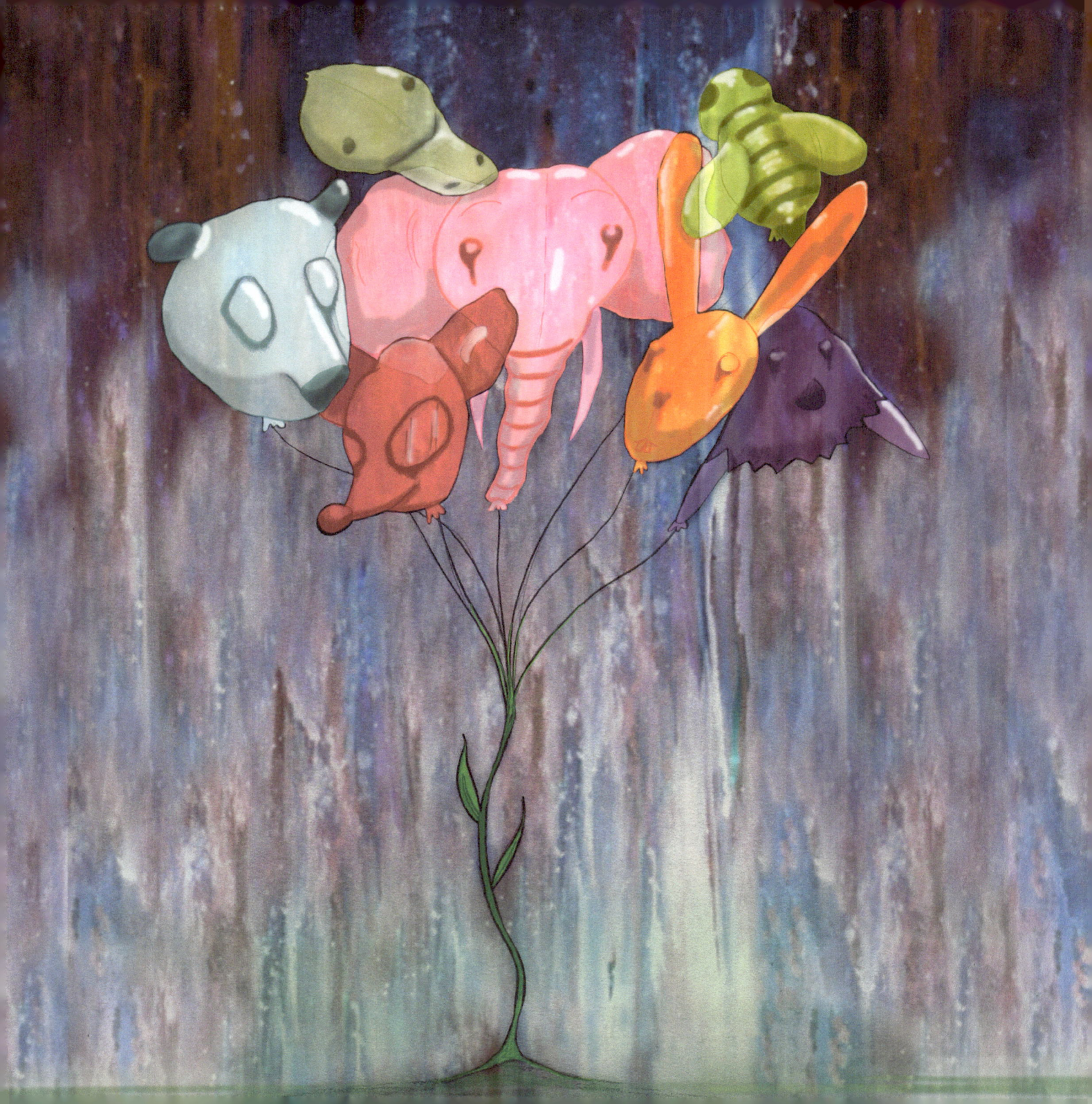

We all know what we are.

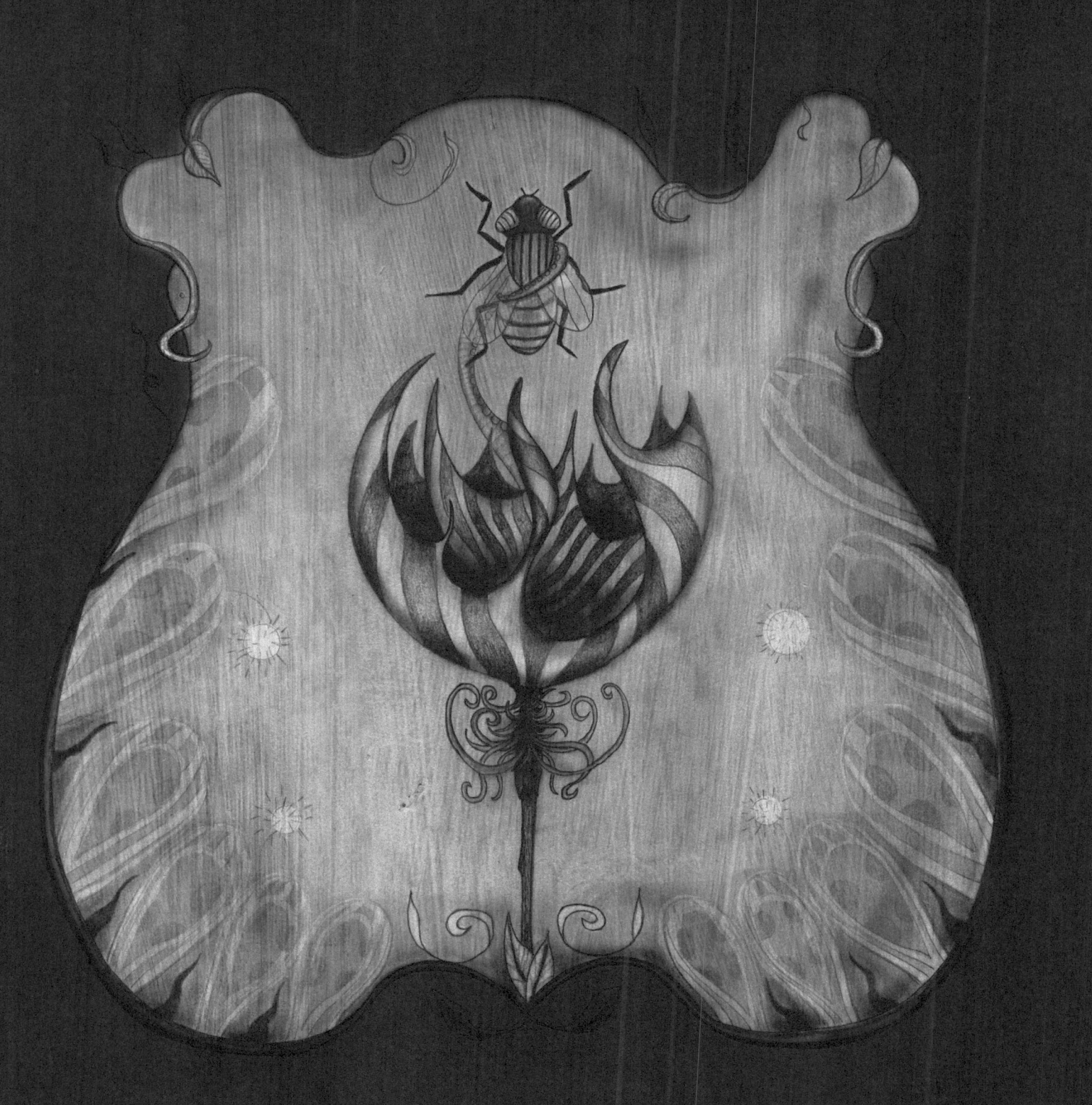

We are the monsters.

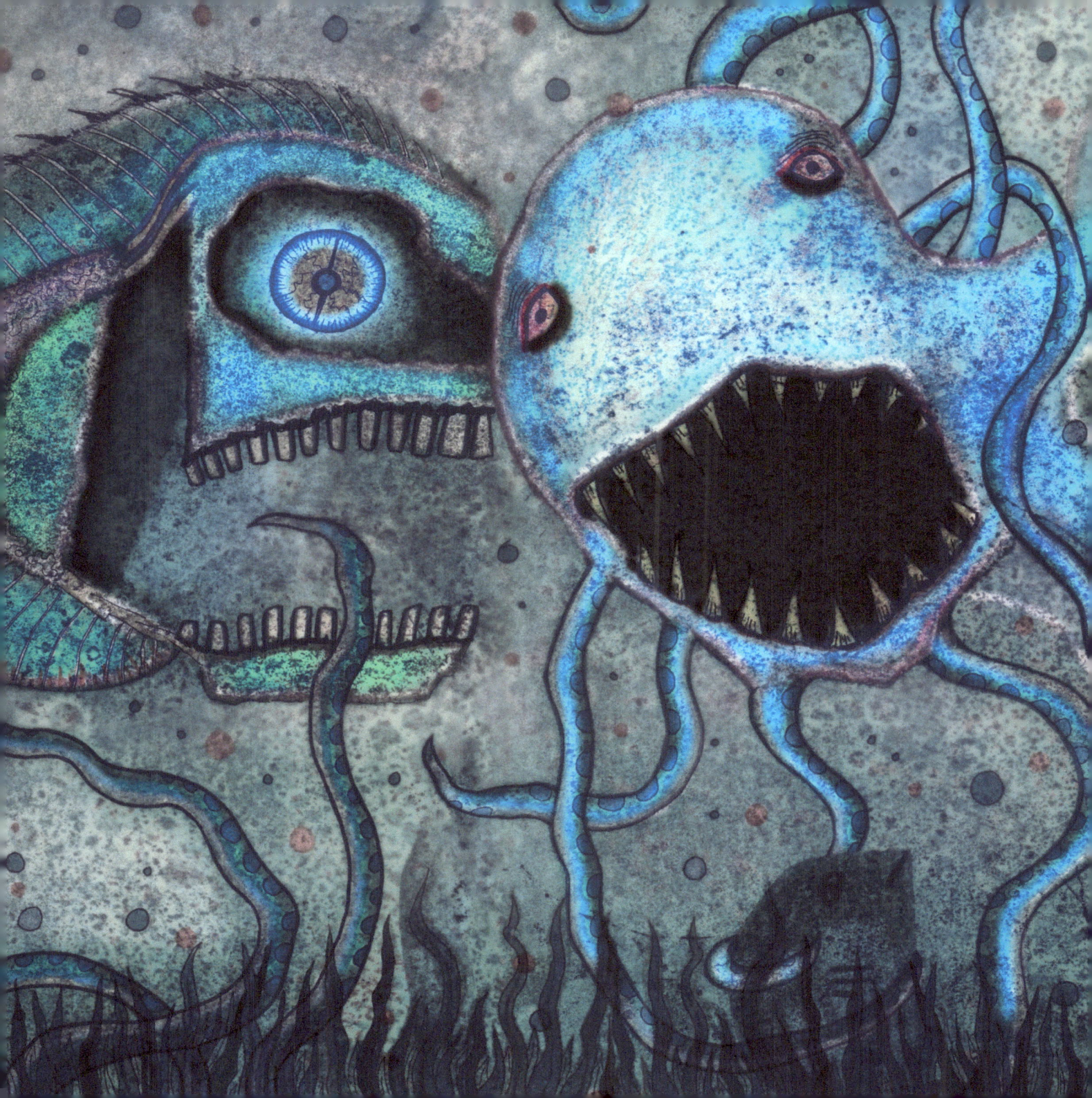

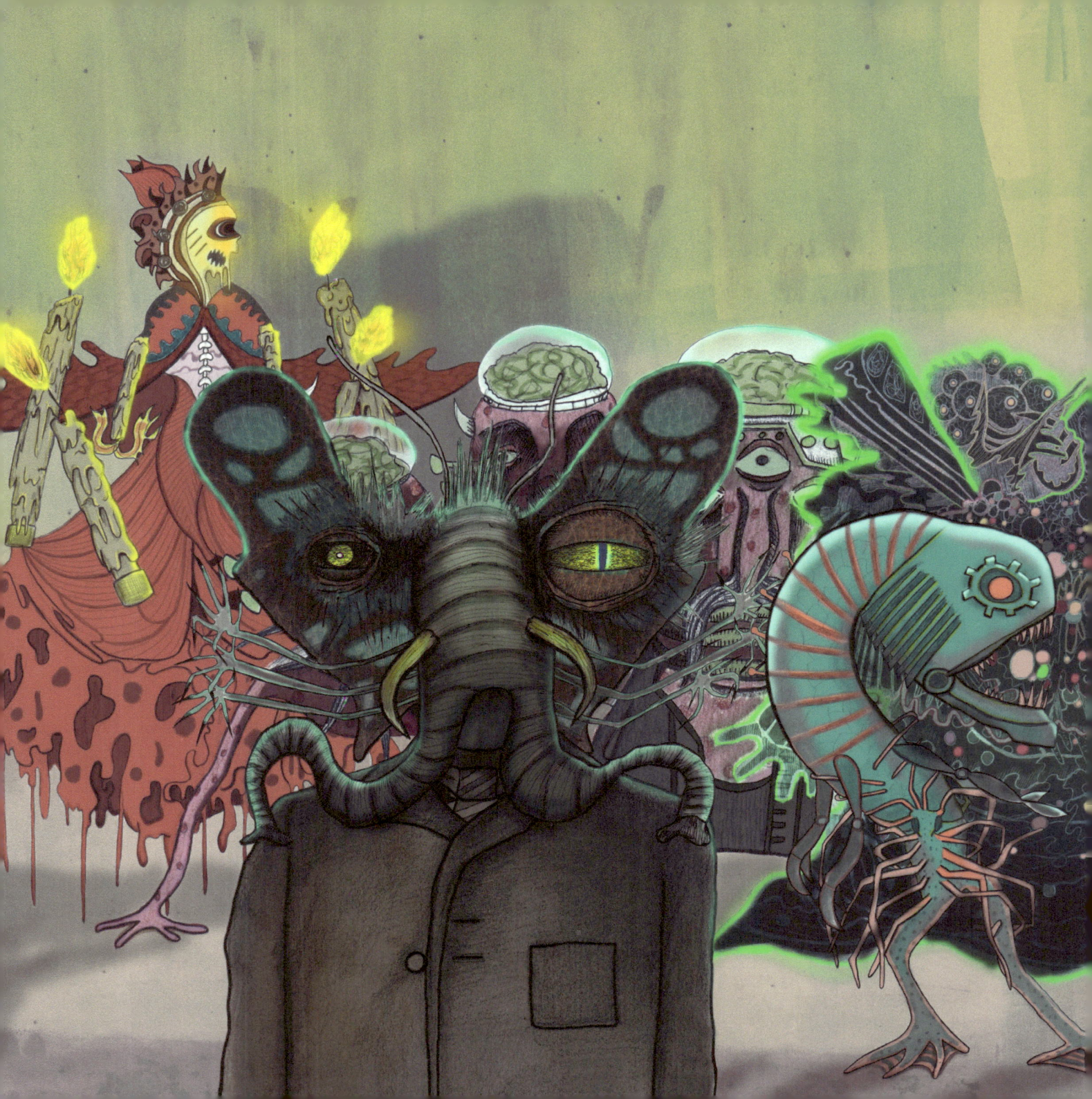

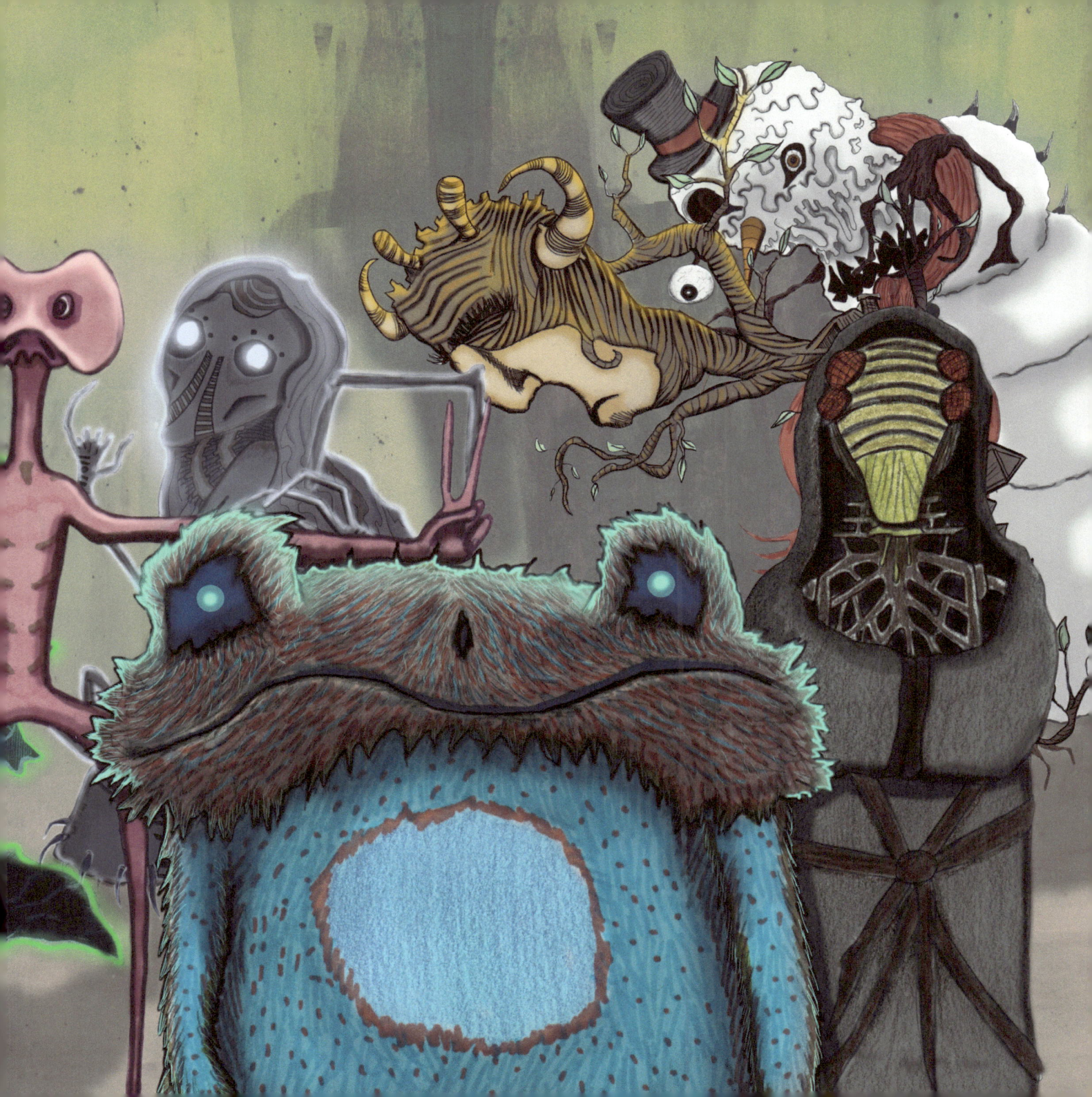

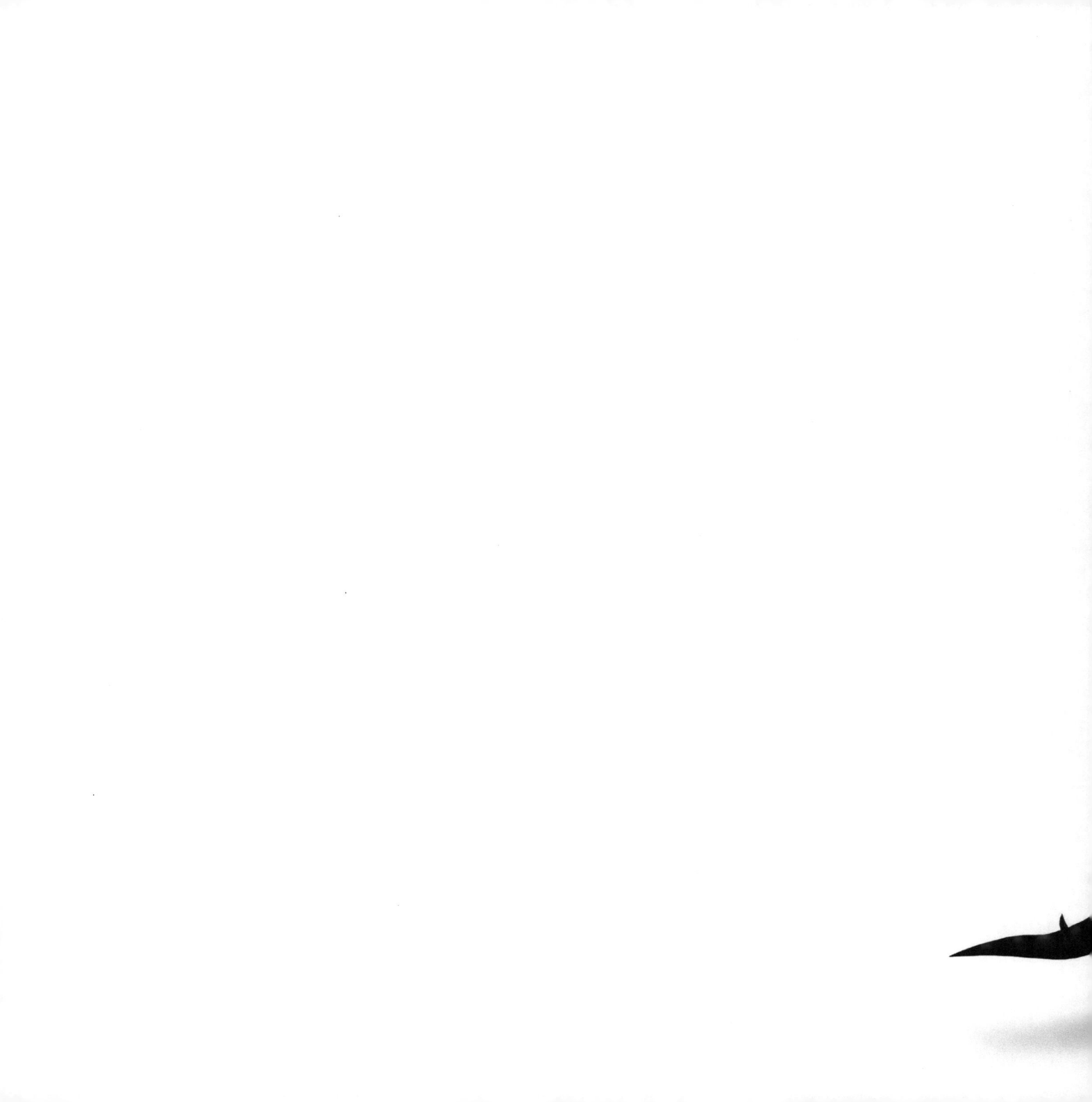

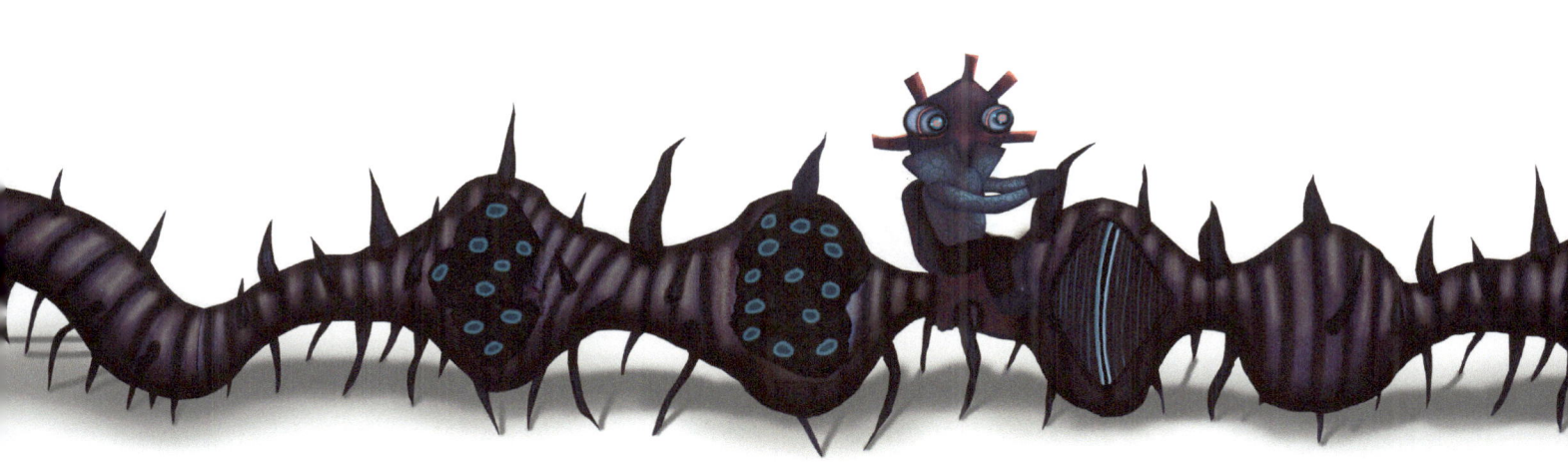

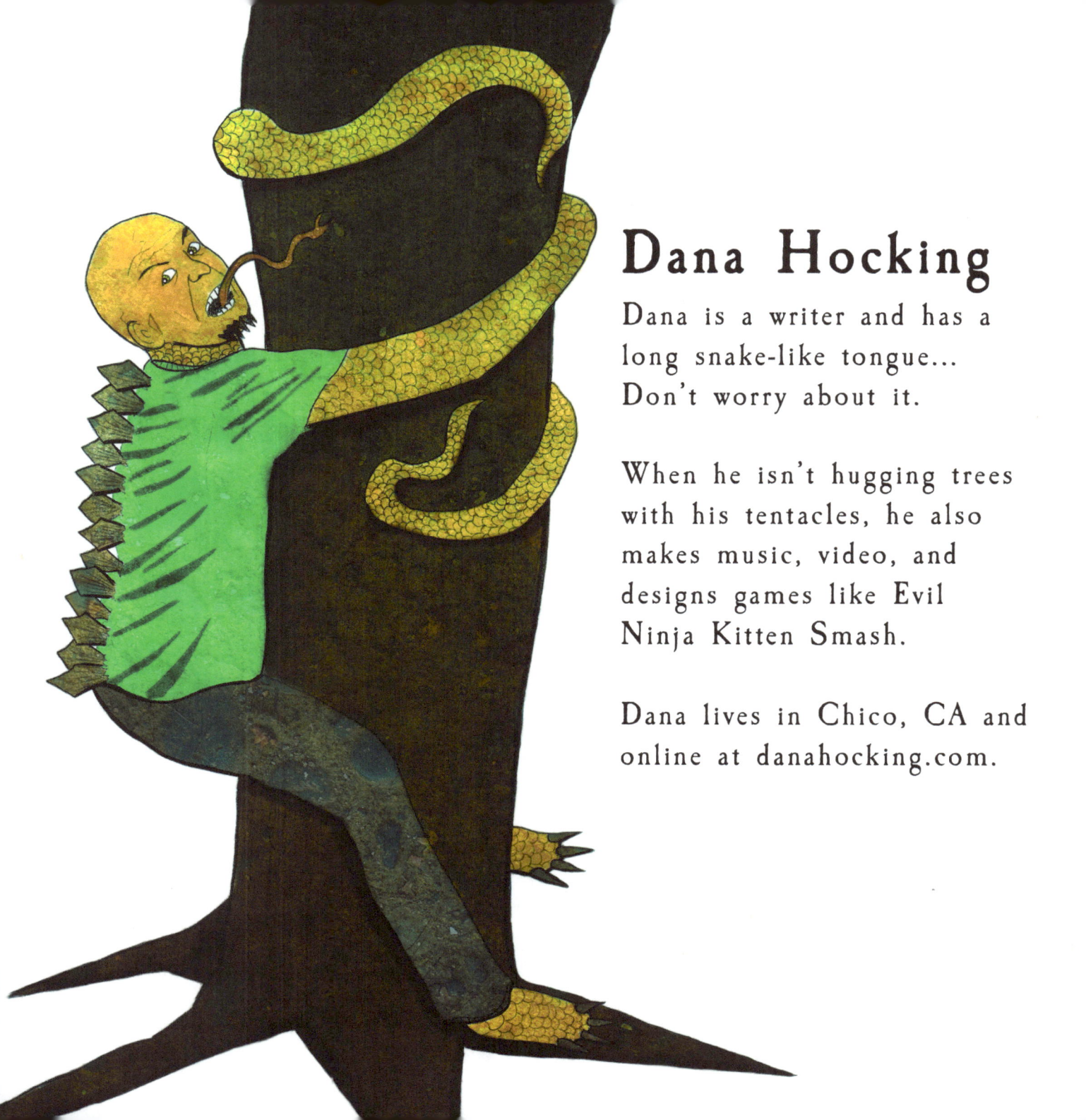

Dana Hocking

Dana is a writer and has a long snake-like tongue... Don't worry about it.

When he isn't hugging trees with his tentacles, he also makes music, video, and designs games like Evil Ninja Kitten Smash.

Dana lives in Chico, CA and online at danahocking.com.

Josh Funk

Josh is an illustrator, filmmaker, and stop-motion animator. He loves fantasy, horror, likable monsters, absurd scenarios, and mixing the bizarre and scary with a little humor.

He is the director of the stop-motion animated film *Wormholes* and the sci-fi space adventure film *The Spaceman*. Josh lives in Chico, CA and online at joshfunk.com.

THANK YOU

To Mommerz. I love you forever.

* * * * * * * * * * * *

To my family and friends who support me, I love you all.
Thank you for your awesomeness and ridiculousness
over the years. You are my favorite monsters.

- Dana

THANK YOU
To Jenny and Jonah, the loves of my life.

* * * * * * * * * * * *

To all of my lovely friends and family, those who
have encouraged my creative appetite, and those who
have challenged me to be better. Thank you for sharing
your wisdom, foolishness, love, and memories.

- Josh

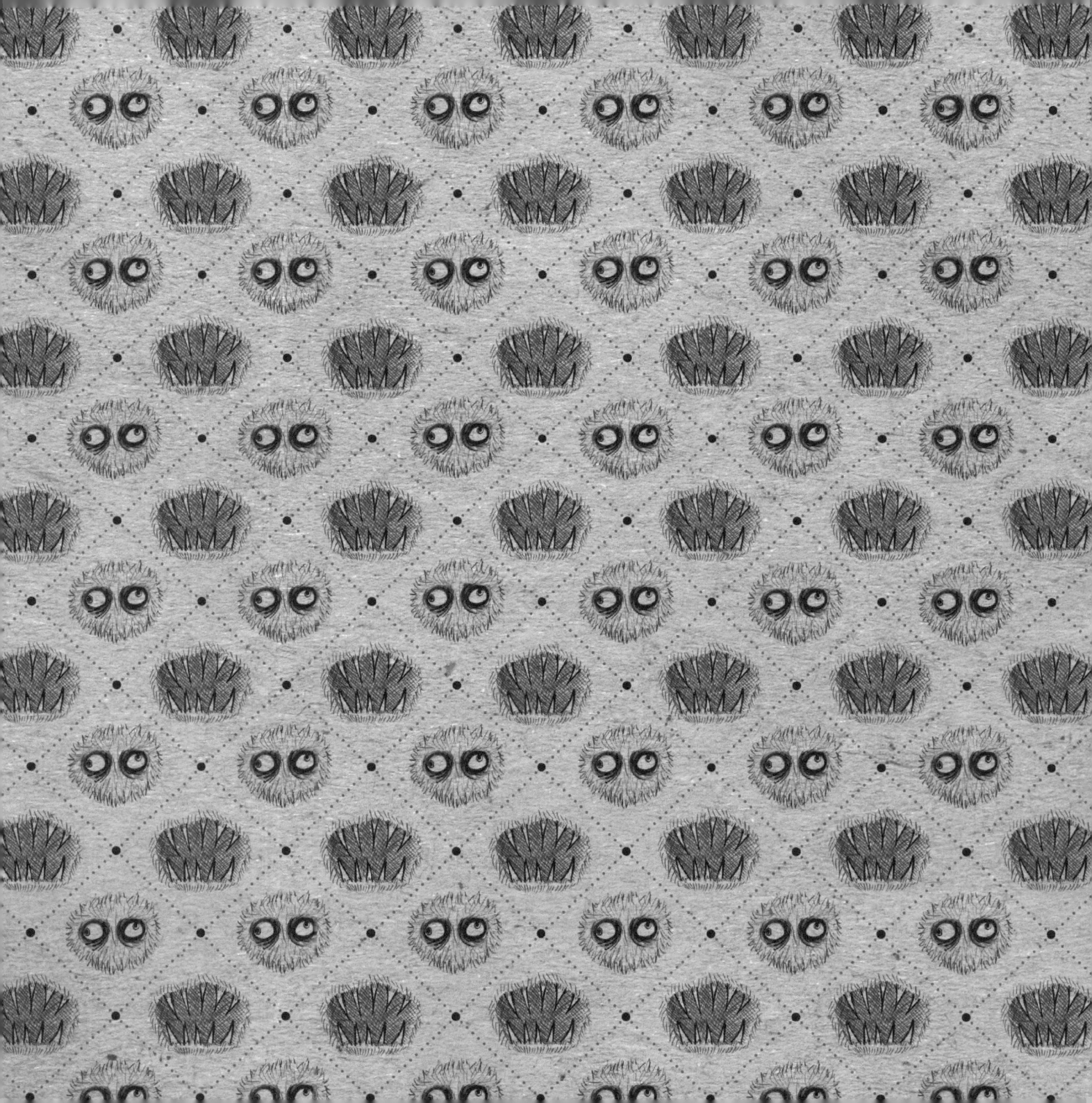

www.ingramcontent.com/pod-product-compliance
Lightning Source LLC
Chambersburg PA
CBHW040748200526
45159CB00023B/1774